GW00506611

Balanced Bread

Bread Machine Recipes

Balanced Bread

Bread Machine Recipes

/ Recipes: Didier Rubio /
/ Photographs: Jean-Pierre Duval /
/ Translation: Anne Trager /

Romain Pages Publishing

A word from the dietician

Bread was the staple food in diets at the beginning of the last century (in 1900, people ate an average of 900g or 2 lb per day per person). Over time, consumption decreased, going from 250g (9oz) in 1960 (a little more than a baguette) to 165g (4¾oz) per day per person in the early 2000s.

The composition of the most common bread has also changed. Previously, barely refined flour was used, giving the bread a brown or grey colour. However, starting in the 1950s, very refined white flours began to be used. Since the Second World War, the resulting white bread has perhaps been more prestigious, but is also very low in fibre and micronutrients (vitamins and minerals), because the latter are found mostly in the wheat bran and germ, which are removed when the flour is refined.

Contrary to popular belief, when bread is eaten in quantities adapted to our needs, it is not fattening. It is more what you put on the bread that makes you gain weight! Bread is not very high in calories (white bread: 255 kcal/100 g or 3½oz; wheat bread: 230 kcal/100 g or 3½oz). It is high in carbohydrates (55% starch), which means that it corresponds perfectly to nutritionist recommendations that 55% of your calorie intake to be in the form of carbohydrates (grains, starches, vegetables and fruit).

Bread truly is a healthy food that should be a part of every meal. Furthermore, it is perfectly adapted to people who do sports.

The goal of this book is to rehabilitate bread as a staple food in our meals, by proposing the alternative of making your own bread with a bread machine. In these pages you will discover original recipes using top quality ingredients.

In these recipes, we favour the use of little refined wholemeal flours and flour made from other grains. As we have mention, they are richer in vitamins, minerals and fibre and, furthermore, they produce bread that has a lower glycemic index than white bread, which is preferable for regulating glycemia (blood sugar levels) and eating behaviour (snacking and cravings for sweets.)

We recommend using organically grown ingredients to limit the intake of pesticides used in intensive farming; they concentrate mainly in the germ and bran, and in the skin of fruit.

In addition to the basic ingredients (flour, water, yeast or starter), the bread variations that you find on these pages also include less common ingredients such as oilseeds (which are rich in good fatty acids, such as omega-3), dried and fresh fruit (rich in soluble fibre, micronutrients, and more), spices, herbs, honey, and the like. These associations result in special breads with original flavours, adapted to daily meals or specifically designed for breakfast, snacks or desserts. You will also find recipes especially adapted to athletes and physically active people.

These recipes are developed by dietitians, so in addition to pleasing the taste buds, they are also nutritionally interesting. The ingredients were chosen not only for their organoleptic qualities (colour, flavour, texture, aroma), but also for dietetic reasons. All the breads in this book are rich in fibre, from the choice of flour, but also thanks to the use of fresh and dried fruit and the oilseeds they contain. This fibre, be it soluble (fruit in general) or insoluble (seeds in general), contributes to a feeling of fullness and to regulating intestinal transit, and it also spreads nutrient absorption over time, regulating blood sugar levels and reducing fat absorption (particularly cholesterol). It also has a protective effect on the digestive tract's epithelium, limiting contact with potentially harmful products (toxins, charred residues, etc.).

Fruits, seeds and plants in general are good to eat, because they are rich in vitamins, minerals (potassium, magnesium, calcium, etc.), trace elements and phytonutrients (which can also be found in certain spices and herbs), such as lycopene, which is found in tomatoes.

These phytoprotective ingredients play an antioxidant role in the body, contributing to neutralising free radicals (components given off when the body's cells break down) which, when produced in excess (due to pollution, stress or sports, for example), have a negative effect on the health.

Finally, many of the oilseeds used in these recipes have fatty acids from the omega-3 family, which have a beneficial effect on the cardiovascular system and help regulate lipaemia (the presence of lipids in the blood). People generally do not eat enough of these omega-3 fatty acids. They can also be found in so-called "oily" fish, such as anchovies.

There you have a number of good reasons to make your own bread with the recipes we propose. It is far from our minds to discredit quality bakers: a good fresh baguette, still warm and crusty, also offers a moment of pleasure. But it should be less frequent than eating wholemeal or brown bread; these you should eat daily, something you can put into practice using this book.

With this book, you will experience more than gustatory pleasure. You will also have the satisfaction of making a noble product with nutritional qualities. Choosing the ingredients and making the bread will make both young and old happy.

Ready, set… to your bread machines!

Abbreviations used for measuring units:
kg: kilogram; g: gram; ml: millilitre; oz: ounce; lb: pound;
fl oz: fluid ounce; tsp: teaspoon; tbsp: tablespoon; c: cup.

Some tricks and details

Bread weight: You can calculate the weight of the loaf by adding the weight of all the dry ingredients to half the weight of the liquid ingredients.

Quantity of liquid: Every machine has its own hydration rate, or ideal ratio between the quantity of liquid (water, milk, eggs, oil) and the quantity of flour. The type of flour used and how humid it is also have an effect. It should be easy to determine your machine's hydration rate under usual conditions of use.

You can calculate the hydration rate by preparing a simple recipe and verifying whether the quantity of water indicated is satisfactory or not. In about ten minutes, it should form a smooth, elastic ball that does not stick to the sides of the bread pan.

If the dough that forms is too dry, add water in small quantities (make sure you measure it precisely). Wait between additions, and add until the ball forms. If, on the other hand, the amount of liquid given in the recipe is too large, add flour in small, precisely measured quantities.

Note down the proportion of liquid to flour, which allows you to figure out your machine's hydration rate, which you can use for other recipes.

– Hydration rate = (quantity of water/quantity of flour) x 100.
– Quantity of water = (hydration rate/100) x quantity of flour.

Always use filtered water: it plays an important role in the bread's final flavour.

Making bread: You machine takes care of the entire process of making, rising and cooking the bread. All you have to do then is let it rest a little while on the rack before tasting it. Make sure you remove the kneading blade quickly, so you do not bite down into it, or possibly throw it out with a leftover piece of bread!

We recommend that you choose a simple recipe and make it several times if necessary until you understand perfectly how your machine works. This will enable you to get to know the hydration rate and the crust colour you prefer, among other things.

Ingredients

Flour: Wheat flour varies with the amount of bran and germ found in the final product. In some countries, such as France, a number indicates the ash mass, or mineral matter that remains after being incinerated, but flour differs greatly from country to country. There are four main types:

> – White flour (soft or pastry flour, plain or all-purpose flour, strong or bread flour, super strong or high gluten flour)
> – Strong brown flour, light whole wheat or 80% or 81% extraction flour
> – Whole meal or whole wheat or 85% to 90% extraction flour
> – Strong whole meal or whole wheat (95% extraction) or very strong 100% whole wheat

The higher up on the scale you go, the richer it is in bran, fibre, vitamins, minerals and trace elements. The translation tries to suggest the closest equivalent to the French flour used in the original recipes.

Baker's yeast: This is the leavening ingredient that goes into bread. It comes in many different forms: cake yeast, active dry yeast and instant yeast. The first two have to be mixed with a little warm liquid before being used—yeast is, in fact, alive and needs to reach a temperature of around 37°C (98.6°F) to be effective; beyond this temperature it can die. Only instant yeast can be put as is in your machine, and it is the yeast form that is best adapted to use in the bread machine. We recommend using it to make the recipes in this book. It can be found in supermarkets, and is often sold in single-dose packets. You can replace it with active dry yeast bought in an organic store. The amount of fresh yeast to use is about one cube (25 g/1 oz) for a loaf that weighs 500 (1 lb 2 oz).

Dehydrated starters: These are dehydrated natural leavens or sourdough starters that can be found in some organic stores and supermarkets. The bread made with a starter rises differently and tastes differently than one made with baker's yeast.

Liquids: You should choose room-temperature or slightly warm liquids (no warmer than 38°C/100.4°F) to make sure the leavening agent acts properly.

Salt: This is an essential ingredient in bread making, giving taste and contributing to making the dough rise properly. Bread requires exact doses of salt: too little will cause it to rise too much and then collapse when cooked, and too much will cause an excessive slow-down in the fermentation process. Always use fine salt (larger grain salt could scratch the loaf pan), and choose unrefined salt. Beware: the yeast or starter should not be in direct contact with the salt before the machine does the kneading, as it will impede the rising process.

Sugar: This also participates in the fermentation process, nourishing the leavening agent and contributing to making the crust golden brown. As a result, a number of recipes contain a small amount of sugar. We recommend using organically grown raw sugar or whole cane sugar.

Other ingredients:
Fat: Breads made with some sort of fat are moister and keep longer. You can use all kinds of fats, but butter and high-quality oils give the best flavour. If you use butter, make sure that you cut it into small pieces so that is will mix evenly throughout the dough.

Milk, dairy products or plant milks: The use of animal or plant milks or other dairy products adds nutritional value to the bread and, of course, changes its taste and consistency. In addition, they have an emulsifying effect, which makes the inside look nice.

Other additions: You can add spices, seeds, fruit, dried or fresh vegetables, bacon, or olives to your bread. Add them at the beginning, especially if using dried spices, or when the machine beeps, which means the ingredients will be mixed for less time and the pieces (say, of fruit) will stay bigger.

Note: If you encounter any problems using your bread machine, we recommend you contact the manufacturer's customer service department, as they will be best placed to give you specific information about your machine.

/ Basic Bread /

Setting: quick bread

Weight: approx. 800 g/1 ¾ lb

Put all the ingredients in the machine's bread pan in the listed order. Choose the setting and the crust colour. Start the machine. At the end of the cycle, remove the bread from the pan and set on a rack to cool.

Ingredients

- 325 ml/11 fl oz/1 ⅓ c filtered water
- 1 ½ tbsp sugar
- 1 ½ tsp *fleur de sel* or fine sea salt
- 20 g/⅔ oz/1 ½ tbsp first cold pressed organic extra virgin olive oil
- 600 g/1 lb 5 oz/4 ⅘ c organic strong brown flour (81% extaction) or light wheat flour
- 1 packet instant yeast

/ This traditional bread goes with any meal, including breadkfast and snack, because the choice of high quality ingredients gives it undeniable nutritional qualities. /

For:
everyone
everyday
every meal

/ wheat flour
/ olive oil

11

/ Mediterranean Bread /

Setting: whole grain bread

Weight: approx. 800 g/1 ¾ lb

Put all the ingredients in the machine's bread pan in the listed order. Choose the setting and the crust colour. Start the machine. At the end of the cycle, remove the bread from the pan and set on a rack to cool.

Ingredients

- 330 ml/11 ⅛ fl oz/1 ⅖ c filtered water
- 2 tbsp first cold pressed organic extra virgin olive oil
- 25 g/1 scant oz/5 tsp whole grain mustard
- 1 ½ tsp herb salt
- 10 g/⅓ oz/1 tbsp fresh or frozen chopped garlic
- 100 g/3 ½ oz/¾ c very strong 100% whole wheat flour
- 500 g/18 oz/4 c organic super strong (high-gluten) flour
- 1 packet instant yeast

/ The ingredients used to make this bread (olive oil, fibre-rich flour) are chosen from among those found in the Mediterranean diet, so well-known for being healthy, and particularly good for the heart. Unfortunately we are moving farther and farther away from these food habits. We recommend you eat this bread with raw or cooked vegetables, such as a tomato salad when it is the season, ratatouille or fish. /

For:
everyone
athletes
the heart

/ wheat flour
/ olive oil
/ garlic

13

/ Carrot-Orange Bread /

Setting: basic bread

Weight: approx. 800 g/1 ¾ lb

Put all the ingredients in the machine's bread pan in the listed order. Choose the setting and the crust colour. Start the machine. At the end of the cycle, remove the bread from the pan and set on a rack to cool.

Ingredients

- 350 ml/12 fl oz/1 ½ c organic carrot-orange juice
- 1 ½ tsp *fleur de sel* or fine sea salt
- 2 tsp organic canola oil
- 2 tsp organic whole cane sugar
- 600 g/1 lb 5 oz/4 ⅘ c organic super strong (high-gluten) flour
- 1 packet instant yeast

/ This bread has a light, airy inside that is a bright orange colour and has a slight carrot taste that goes perfectly with meals. Carrot and orange contain beta-carotene, which has powerful antioxidant powers and is good for the skin and the eyes. /

For:

vacationers
the sun

/ Omega-3 Bread /

Setting: whole grain bread

Weight: approx. 800 g/1 ¾ lb

Put all the ingredients in the machine's bread pan in the listed order. Choose the setting and the crust colour. Start the machine. At the end of the cycle, remove the bread from the pan and set on a rack to cool.

Ingredients

- 350 ml/12 fl oz/1 ½ c filtered water
- 1 ½ tsp *fleur de sel* or fine sea salt
- 2 ½ tbsp first cold pressed organic walnut oil
- 1 tsp organic whole cane sugar
- 400 g/14 oz/3 c very strong (high-gluten) flour
- 200 g/7 oz/1 ½ c very strong 100% whole wheat flour
- 60 g/2 oz/½ c chopped walnuts
- 1 packet instant yeast

/ Walnut oil makes this bread rich in polyunsaturated fatty acids, and especially in omega-3, which contributes to reducing LDL or "bad" cholesterol and helps fluidify the blood. The body does not know how to make it, so this bread can be eaten daily as a source of this essential fatty acid. This bread is ideal for breakfast, at meals and for snack. /

For:

everyone
everyday
cheese lovers

/ Mixed Seed Bread /

Setting: whole grain bread

Weight: approx. 800 g/1 ¾ lb

Put all the ingredients in the machine's bread pan in the listed order. Choose the setting and the crust colour. Start the machine. At the end of the cycle, remove the bread from the pan and set on a rack to cool.

Ingredients

- 330 ml/11 ⅕ fl oz/1 ⅖ c filtered water
- 2 ½ tbsp organic corn oil
- 1 ½ tsp *fleur de sel* or fine sea salt
- 200 g/7 oz/1 ½ c organic mixed grain or five-grain flour
- 200 g/7 oz/1 ½ c very strong (high gluten) flour
- 200 g/7 oz/1 ½ c strong brown flour (81% extaction) or light wheat flour
- 1 tablet vitamin C
- 100 g/3 ½ oz/¾ cup sunflower, poppy, squash and sesame seeds
- 1 packet instant yeast

/ This mixed seed bread is ideal for breakfast and snacktime, but can also be enjoyed served with salad and cheese. The mixture of various flours and seeds gives this loaf a concentration of nutritional elements, including magnesium, potassium and good fatty acids. Do not hesitate to try other seeds. /

For:

everyone
athletes

/ Open Sesame /

Setting: basic bread

Weight: approx. 1 kg/2.2 lb

Put all the ingredients in the machine's bread pan in the listed order. Choose the setting and the crust colour. Start the machine. At the end of the cycle, remove the bread from the pan and set on a rack to cool.

Ingredients

- 325 ml/11 fl oz/1 ⅓ c filtered water
- 2 tbsp organic sesame oil
- 5 tsp gomashio
- 40 g/1 ½ oz organic sesame paste
- 10 g/⅓ oz/1 tsp organic raw cane sugar
- 50 g/1 ¾ oz/⅜ c organic very strong 100% whole wheat flour
- 550 g/1 lb 4 oz/4 ⅜ c organic strong brown flour (81% extraction) or light whole wheat flour
- 1 packet instant yeast

/ This bread is made entirely from organically grown ingredients chosen for their magnesium, fibre and omega-6 essential fatty acids, which are found in sesame. It contains sesame paste, which means it needs no added oil, and the gomashio (toasted sesame ground with sea salt) gives a light, one-of-a-kind flavour. /

For:
intestinal transit
stress
the heart

/ Walnut and Hazelnut Bread /

Setting: basic bread

Weight: approx. 850 g/1 lb 12 oz

Ingredients

- 330 ml/11 ⅕ fl oz/1 ⅖ c warm filtered water
- 1 tbsp organic squash seed oil
- 1 tbsp organic canola oil
- 1 tbs four-oil blend such as Isio 4
- 1 ½ tsp fine sea salt
- 100 g/3 ½ oz/⅞ c organic strong brown flour (81% extraction) or light whole wheat flour
- 500 g/18 oz/4 c organic strong whole meal flour, 95% extraction (dark whole wheat flour)
- 60 g/2 oz/½ c chopped hazelnuts
- 60 g/2 oz/½ c chopped walnuts
- 1 packet instant yeast

Put all the ingredients in the machine's bread pan in the listed order. Choose the setting and the crust colour. Start the machine. At the end of the cycle, remove the bread from the pan and set on a rack to cool.

/ This bread is rich in essential fatty acids and can be eaten daily, because it has omega-3 to balance out omega-6 fatty acids, which we usually eat too much of. /

For:

everyone
everyday
every meal

/ wheat flout
/ hazelnuts
/ walnuts

21

/ Walnut Bread /

Setting: whole grain bread

Weight: approx. 850 g/1 lb 12 oz

Put all the ingredients in the machine's bread pan in the listed order. Choose the setting and the crust colour. Start the machine. At the end of the cycle, remove the bread from the pan and set on a rack to cool.

Ingredients

- 325 ml/11 fl oz/1 ⅓ c filtered water
- 1 ½ tsp *fleur de sel* or fine sea salt
- 2 tbsp first cold pressed organic walnut oil
- 400 g/14 oz/3 ½ c organic strong brown flour (81% extraction) or light whole wheat flour
- 200 g/7 oz/1 ½ c organic dark rye flour
- 100 g/3 ½ oz/⅘ c chopped walnuts
- 1 packet instant yeast

/ With the full flavour of walnut pieces, this bread goes well toasted for breakfast or served along with salad and cheeses. The walnuts and walnut oil contain omega-3 polyunsaturated fatty acids, which are essential for the body. /

For:
cheese lovers
the heart
everyday

/ wheat flour
/ walnut oil
/ walnuts

23

/ Calming Bread /

Setting: basic bread

Weight: approx. 800 g/1 ¾ lb

Put all the ingredients in the machine's bread pan in the listed order. Choose the setting and the crust colour. Start the machine. At the end of the cycle, remove the bread from the pan and set on a rack to cool.

Ingredients

- 330 ml/11 ⅕ fl oz/1 ⅔ c filtered water
- 1 ½ tsp *fleur de sel* or fine sea salt
- 35 ml/1 ⅕ fl oz/7 tsp hemp oil
- 1 tbsp organic whole cane sugar
- 200 g/7 oz/1 ½ c very strong 100% whole wheat flour
- 400 g/14 oz/3 ½ c organic super strong (high-gluten) flour
- 70 g/2 ½ oz organic poppy seeds
- 1 packet instant yeast

/ Poppy seeds give this spotted bread a crunch. It can be eaten with every meal. Hemp oil is rich in polyunsaturated fatty acids that have a good omega-6/omega-3 ratio, which helps fight aging and cardiovascular diseases, and also softens the skin. The oil has only tiny quantities of euphoria-producing substances. /

For:

everyone
stress

/ Barley Bread /

Setting: basic bread

Weight: approx. 1 kg/2.2 lb

Put all the ingredients in the machine's bread pan in the listed order. Choose the setting and the crust colour. Start the machine. At the end of the cycle, remove the bread from the pan and set on a rack to cool.

Ingredients

- 330 ml/11 ⅛ fl oz/1 ⅖ c filtered water
- 4 tbsp first cold pressed organic extra virgin olive oil
- 1 ½ tsp fine table salt
- 3 tbsp organic whole cane sugar
- 400 g/14 oz/3 ½ c organic brown barley flour (80–82% extraction)
- 200 g/7 oz/1 ½ c organic strong brown flour (81% extraction) or light whole wheat flour
- 1 packet instant yeast

/ This bread is made mainly with barley flour, which is rich in fibre (beta-glucan) that can lower LDL cholesterol (the "bad" cholesterol). This very full bread makes you feel full quickly. /

For:
hunger
arteries

/ Wheat Germ Bread /

Setting: whole grain bread

Weight: approx. 800 g/1 ¾ lb

Put all the ingredients in the machine's bread pan in the listed order. Choose the setting and the crust colour. Start the machine. At the end of the cycle, remove the bread from the pan and set on a rack to cool.

Ingredients

- 330 ml/11 ⅓ fl oz/1 ⅔ c filtered water
- 1 ½ tsp *fleur de sel* or fine sea salt
- 2 ½ tbsp first cold pressed organic extra virgin olive oil
- 2 tsp organic whole cane sugar
- 100 g/3 ½ oz/¾ c de germes de blé
- 400 g/14 oz/3 ½ c organic strong brown flour (81% extraction) or light whole wheat flour
- 100 g/3 ½ oz/¾ c dark rye flour
- 1 packet instant yeast

/ This bread is nutritionally interesting for its B vitamins and its minerals such as magnesium and phosphorus. It also has a high concentration of vitamin E, which is a natural antioxydant, and it is rich in trace elements like iron, copper and zinc. /

For:

everyone
everyday

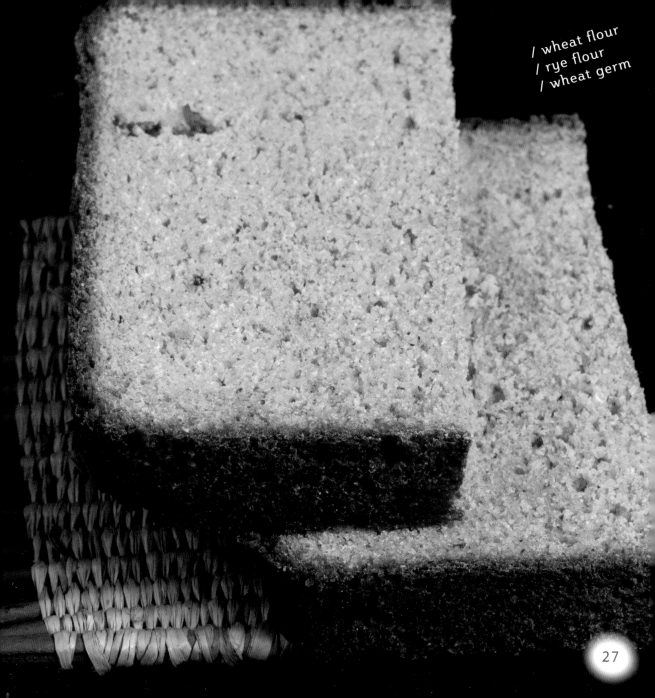

27

/ Iron Bread /

Setting: whole grain bread

Weight: approx. 850 g/1 lb 14 oz

Ingredients

- 340 ml/11 ½ fl oz/1 ⅖ c plus 2 tsp filtered water
- 2 ½ tsp organic sunflower oil
- 1 ½ tsp *fleur de sel* or fine sea salt
- 5 g/⅕ oz/2 sheets nori (seaweed)
- 100 g/3 ½ oz/¾ cup pistachios, squash and sunflower seeds
- 420 g/15 oz/heaped 3 ½ c organic super strong (high-gluten) flour
- 40 g/1 ½ oz/4 tbsp organic buckwheat flour
- 60 g/2 oz/½ c organic lupine flour
- 80 g/2 ⅘ oz/⅔ c organic strong whole meal flour, 95% extraction (dark whole wheat flour)
- 1 packet instant yeast

Put all the ingredients in the machine's bread pan in the listed order. Choose the setting and the crust colour. Start the machine. At the end of the cycle, remove the bread from the pan and set on a rack to cool.

/ Nori is seaweed that contains a variety of minerals and trace elements. This is a very nourishing bread that goes well with lunch and dinner. It is particularly high in plant-derived iron. This kind of iron is harder to assimilate than that of animal origin, so it is recommended that you eat food that is rich in vitamin C at the same meal, such as kiwi or citrus fruit or parsley, because it will help you assimilate the iron. /

For:

pregnant women
athletes
anaemic people

/ wheat flour
/ buckwheat flour
/ lupine flour

29

/ Onion-Vegetable Bread /

Setting: basic bread

Weight: approx. 800 g/1 ¾ lb

Put all the ingredients in the machine's bread pan in the listed order. Choose the setting and the crust colour. Start the machine. At the end of the cycle, remove the bread from the pan and set on a rack to cool.

Ingredients

- 200 ml/6 ⅔ fl oz/⅘ c organic vegetable juice (tomato, celery, beetroot, etc.)
- 130 ml/4 ⅖ fl oz/½ c plus 2 tsp filtered water
- 7 tsp gomashio
- 450 g/1 lb/3 ⅝ c strong brown flour (81% extaction) or light wheat flour
- 130 g/4 ½ oz/1 c organic 85% extraction whole wheat flour
- 120 g/4 ¼ oz/1 c onions, cooked until soft in 20 ml/4 tsp first cold pressed organic extra virgin olive oil
- 1/2 packet instant yeast

/ The vegetable juice gives this bread a very red-orange colour. The onions cooked in olive oil, chosen for its monounsaturated fatty acids, give the bread a slightly sweet taste. This bread is delicious at every meal, and perfectly adapted to making hors-d'oeuvres, spread with a fresh goat or sheep's milk cheese. /

For:

hors-d'oeuvres
meals

/ Roquefort-Walnut Bread /

Setting: whole grain bread

Weight: approx. 1 kg/2.2 lb

Put all the ingredients in the machine's bread pan in the listed order. Choose the setting and the crust colour. Start the machine. At the end of the cycle, remove the bread from the pan and set on a rack to cool.

Ingredients

- 325 ml/11 fl oz/1 ⅓ c filtered water
- 1 ½ tsp *fleur de sel* or fine sea salt
- 2 ½ tbsp first cold pressed organic walnut oil
- 2 tbsp organic whole cane sugar
- 450 g/1 lb/3 ⅝ c organic super strong (high-gluten) flour
- 150 g/4 ¼ oz/1 ¼ c organic dark rye flour
- 80 g/2 ⅘ oz/⅔ c chopped walnuts
- 80 g/2 ⅘ oz/¾ c crumbled roquefort
- 1 packet instant yeast

/ This is a particularly high-energy bread thanks to the roquefort cheese and walnuts, which are rich in lipids. It is delicious served with meals to accompany salad and cheese, or simply toasted as an hors-d'oeuvre. It has a lot of omega-3 essential fatty acids, which are good for the cardiovascular system. /

For:

the heart
intestinal transit
roquefort lovers

/ Traditional Sourdough Bread /

Setting: basic bread

Weight: approx. 750 g/1 ⅔ lb

Put all the ingredients in the machine's bread pan in the listed order. Choose the setting and the crust colour. Start the machine. At the end of the cycle, remove the bread from the pan and set on a rack to cool.

Ingredients

- 325 ml/11 fl oz/1 ⅓ c filtered water
- 2 ½ tbsp organic sunflower oil
- 1 tsp fine table salt
- 2 tbsp white sugar
- 600 g/1 lb 5 oz/4 ⅘ c organic strong brown flour (81% extaction) or light wheat flour
- 25 g/1 oz organic starter

/ Starter is made from flour and water and causes a slower fermentation. As a result, the bread keeps longer, but is also more flavourful and helps the body better absorb and use the micronutrients found in the bread. /

For:

everyone
everday
every meal

/ Quick Bread /

Put all the ingredients in the machine's bread pan in the listed order. Choose the setting and the crust colour. Start the machine. At the end of the cycle, remove the bread from the pan and set on a rack to cool.

Ingredients

- 170 ml/5 ¾ fl oz/scant ¾ c organic vegetable stock (water + bouillon cube)
- 2 tsp organic whole cane sugar
- 2 tbsp organic oil of your choice
- 300 g/10 ½ oz/2 ½ c organic flour of your choice
- ½ packet instant yeast

/ This simple little bread goes with meals everyday. It can be made with various types of flour and oils, which means it can be made to use up bread-making ingredients you have in your pantry. The use of organic vegetable stock gives a pleasent flavour and means you do not have to add salt. /

For:

everyday
every meal
people in a hurry

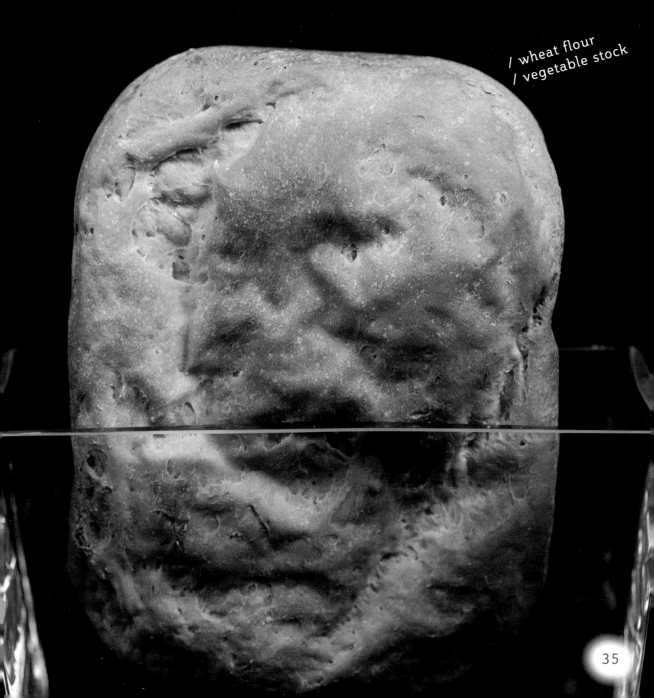

35

/ Lovers' Bread /

Setting: basic bread

Weight: approx. 850 g/1 lb 14 oz

Put all the ingredients in the machine's bread pan in the listed order. Choose the setting and the crust colour. Start the machine. At the end of the cycle, remove the bread from the pan and set on a rack to cool.

Ingredients

- 330 ml/11 ⅓ fl oz/1 ⅔ c filtered water
- 4 tbsp first cold pressed organic extra virgin olive oil
- 1 tsp fine table salt
- 1 ½ tbsp honey
- 1 pinch ground Espelette or other medium chilli
- 500 g/18 oz/4 c organic super strong (high-gluten) flour
- 100 g/3 ½ oz/⅞ c organic strong brown flour (81% extaction) or light wheat flour
- 30 to 40 g/1 to 1 ½ oz chopped candied ginger
- 30 g/1 oz capers
- 1 packet instant yeast

/ The chilli pepper, capers and ginger found in this bread are said to have aphrodisiac effect. Try it out. It is delicious as an hors-d'oeuvre and served with cheese. /

/ You can replace a third of the water with 100 ml/3 ⅓ fl oz/⅖ c ginger juice. Make ginger juice by grating a piece of fresh ginger the size of a small Belgian endive and remove the zest of two juicy lemons. Place the ginger in a bowl or bottle and cover with 100 ml/3 ⅓ fl oz/⅖ c water. Leave to macerate for 8 hours. Strain to recuperate the juice. Add the lemon juice and around 50 g/1 ¾ oz/3 tbsp sugar. Depending on what your taste, you can add more or less sugar and the zest of one orange. /

For:
adults
lovers
Valentines

/ wheat flour
/ chilli
/ ginger
/ capers

37

/ Oriental Bread /

Setting: basic bread

Weight: approx. 700 g/1 ½ lb

Ingredients

- 250 ml/8 ½ fl oz/1 c filtered water
- 1 ½ tsp table salt
- 1 tsp organic whole cane sugar
- 2 tsp first cold pressed organic extra virgin olive oil
- 1 pinch ground coriander
- 1 pinch ground paprika
- 1 pinch ground cinnamon
- 100 g/3 ½ oz/½ c organic hard wheat semolina
- 250 g/9 oz/1 ½ c plus 5 tbsp organic corn meal
- 50 g/1 ¾ oz/1 c freshly grated carrots
- 50 g/1 ¾ oz/¼ c cooked chickpeas
- 50 g/1 ¾ oz/¼ c dried tomatoes
- 1 packet instant yeast

Put all the ingredients in the machine's bread pan in the listed order. Choose the setting and the crust colour. Start the machine. At the end of the cycle, remove the bread from the pan and set on a rack to cool.

/ This bread, with its subtle oriental flavours, is very complete and rich in fibre and magnesium. In addition, the chickpeas associated with the starches (corn meal and wheat semolina) provide organic, good quality plant proteins. /

For:
everyone
vegetarians
athletes

/ corn meal
/ semolina
/ vegetables
/ spices

39

/ Beer Bread /

Setting: whole grain bread

Weight: approx. 750 g/1 ⅔ lb

Put all the ingredients in the machine's bread pan in the listed order. Choose the setting and the crust colour. Start the machine. At the end of the cycle, remove the bread from the pan and set on a rack to cool.

Ingredients

- 250 ml/8 ½ fl oz/1 c light ale (2.5°)
- 70 ml/2 ⅓ fl oz/¼ c filtered water
- 1 ½ tsp *fleur de sel* or fine sea salt
- 2 tbsp oranic whole cane sugar
- 10 g/⅓ oz/1 scant tbsp organic corn oil
- 10 g/⅓ oz/1 scant tbsp organic sun-flower oil
- 600 g/1 lb 5 oz/4 ⅘ c organic strong brown flour (81% extaction) or light wheat flour
- 1 tsp instant yeast

/ This bread, which is made with a light ale with a very low alcohol content, is moist and delicious. Its corn and sunflower oils provide essential fatty acids and vitamin E, and the beer has vitamin B9. /

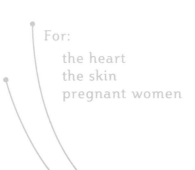

For:
the heart
the skin
pregnant women

/ Squash Seed and Corn Bread /

Setting: basic bread

Weight: approx. 1 kg/2.2 lb

Put all the ingredients in the machine's bread pan in the listed order. Choose the setting and the crust colour. Start the machine. At the end of the cycle, remove the bread from the pan and set on a rack to cool.

Ingredients

- 330 ml/11 ⅕ fl oz/1 ⅔ c filtered water
- 4 tbsp organic squash seed oil
- 1 ½ tsp fine table salt
- 500 g/18 oz/4 c organic spelt flour, 80% to 82% extraction
- 100 g/3 ½ oz/¾ c organic corn meal
- 1 packet instant yeast

/ Squash seeds contain a lot of essential fatty acids and are very effective in preventing cystitis. This basic bread combines spelt and corn and is good for people who do not want to eat too many wheat-based products. /

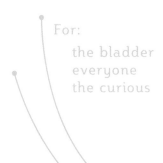

For:
the bladder
everyone
the curious

/ Bacon-Onion Bread /

Setting: basic bread

Weight: approx. 1 kg/2.2 lb

Put all the ingredients in the machine's bread pan in the listed order. Choose the setting and the crust colour. Start the machine. At the end of the cycle, remove the bread from the pan and set on a rack to cool.

Ingredients

- 300 ml/10 fl oz/1 ¼ c filtered water
- 1 tsp fine table salt
- 1 tsp organic whole cane sugar
- 375 g/13 ¼ oz/3 ⅛ c organic strong brown flour (81% extaction) or light wheat flour
- 175 g/6 oz/heaped 1 ¼ c organic super strong (high-gluten) flour
- 30 g/1 oz/⅛ c sunflower seeds
- 100 g/3 ½ oz/⅔ c chopped onions cooked until soft with 3 ½ oz/½ c diced bacon (do not add oil), cooled
- 1 packet instant yeast

/ This bread is excellent when toasted and goes well with meals among friends and for hors-d'oeuvres, cut into cubes. Its flavours will please food lovers' taste buds. Do not eat it everyday, because of its fat content! /

Friend:
food lovers
bon vivants
drinks with friends

/ wheat flour
/ bacon
/ onions

43

/ Italian Bread /

Setting: basic bread

Weight: approx. 800 g/1 ¾ lb

Put all the ingredients in the machine's bread pan in the listed order. Choose the setting and the crust colour. Start the machine. At the end of the cycle, remove the bread from the pan and set on a rack to cool.

Ingredients

- 320 ml/10 ⅘ fl oz/1 ⅓ c filtered water
- 1 tsp table salt
- 1 tsp organic whole cane sugar
- 50 g/1 ¾ oz dried oil-marinated tomatoes, drained
- 1/2 tsp chopped fresh basil
- 60 g/2 oz pitted black olives
- 250 g/9 oz/2 c organic strong brown flour (81% extaction) or light wheat flour
- 250 g/9 oz/2 c organic super strong (high-gluten) flour
- 1 packet instant yeast

/ This bread has Mediterranean flavours that are perfect for a barbecue with friends. You can also cut it into small cubes for a summer hors-d'oeuvre. It is also nutritionally interesting because the dried tomatoes contain lycopene, which is a powerful antioxidant, and the black olives are rich in monounsaturated fatty acids. /

For:

food lovers
meals with friends
theme-based meals

/ Southwestern Bread /

Setting: basic bread

Weight: approx. 800 g/1 ¾ lb

Put all the ingredients in the machine's bread pan in the listed order. Choose the setting and the crust colour. Start the machine. At the end of the cycle, remove the bread from the pan and set on a rack to cool.

Ingredients

- 325 ml/11 fl oz/1 ⅓ c filtered water
- 1 tsp organic whole cane sugar
- 1 tsp *fleur de sel* or fine sea salt
- 20 g/⅔ oz/1 tbsp duck fat
- 600 g/1 lb 5 oz/4 ⅘ c organic strong brown flour (81% extaction) or light wheat flour
- 100 g/3 ½ oz dried duck breast, sliced
- 1 packet instant yeast

/ This bread is reminiscent of Southwestern France and goes deliciously with festive meals and cocktails. The fat it contains (duck fat and duck breast) is rich in monounsaturated fatty acids, which are recognized to be good for the cardiovascular system. Surprise your friends by serving it spread with honey and topped with dried tomatoes. /

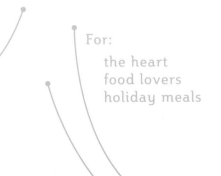

For:
the heart
food lovers
holiday meals

/ wheat flour
/ duck breast

/ Prune Bread /

Setting: basic bread

Weight: approx. 1 kg/2.2 lb

Put all the ingredients in the machine's bread pan in the listed order. Choose the setting and the crust colour. Start the machine. At the end of the cycle, remove the bread from the pan and set on a rack to cool.

Ingredients

- 220 ml/7 ½ fl oz/1 c minus 2 tbsp prune juice
- 120 ml/4 fl oz/½ c filtered water
- 1 ½ tsp *fleur de sel* or fine sea salt
- 3 tbsp organic whole cane sugar
- 600 g/1 lb 5 oz/4 ⅘ c organic strong brown flour (81% extaction) or light wheat flour
- 300 g/10 ½ oz/2 c organic, pitted prunes, in pieces
- 1 packet instant yeast

/ This tender, moist bread is naturally sweetened by the fructose found in the prunes. It is delicious for breakfast, snack time and served with cheese. It is rich in soft fibres, easy to digest, and is full of potassium and magnesium. The prunes will stimulate a lazy digestive tract. /

For:

lazy intestines
athletes
cheese lovers

/ B9 Bread /

Setting: basic bread

Weight: approx. 800 g/1 ¾ lb

Put all the ingredients in the machine's bread pan in the listed order. Choose the setting and the crust colour. Start the machine. At the end of the cycle, remove the bread from the pan and set on a rack to cool.

Ingredients

- 200 ml/6 ⅔ fl oz/⅘ c Nutrinoisette (a hazelnut-based drink)
- 140 ml/4 ¾ fl oz/⅔ c organic, calcium-enriched soy milk
- 1 ½ tsp chestnut honey
- 2 tsp first cold pressed organic hazelnut oil
- 1 tsp table salt
- 150 g/5 ¼ oz/1 ¼ c organic chestnut flour
- 450 g/1 lb/3 ⅝ c organic super strong (high-gluten) flour
- 20 g/⅔ oz/scant ½ c wheat germ
- 20 g/⅔ oz/scant ¼ c fresh hazelnuts
- 1 packet instant yeast

/ This bread is for autumn, with its rich hazelnut base and chestnut honey sweetness. Its originality comes from the choice of main liquid, the oil, and also the flours used, notably the chestnut flour. It is particularly rich in vitamin B9, which is very good for vascular protection. /

For:
the heart
pregnant women
squirrels

/ Fig-Walnut Bread /

Setting: basic bread

Weight: approx. 1 kg/2.2 lb

Put all the ingredients in the machine's bread pan in the listed order. Choose the setting and the crust colour. Start the machine. At the end of the cycle, remove the bread from the pan and set on a rack to cool.

Ingredients

- 350 ml/12 fl oz/1 ½ c filtered water
- 1 tsp table salt
- 1 tsp organic whole cane sugar
- 1 tsp honey
- 500 g/18 oz/4 c organic strong brown flour (81% extaction) or light wheat flour
- 40 g/1 ½ oz/⅓ c chopped fresh walnuts
- 90 g/3 oz/scant ⅔ c dried figs, soaked
- 1 packet instant yeast

/ This slightly sweet bread makes a fine addition to holiday tables. It is ideal served with foie gras and hard cheeses, creating a subtle blend of flavours. It is also interesting nutritionally for its fibers and omega-3 fatty acids. /

For:

food lovers
holiday meals
lazy intestines

/ Fig Bread /

Setting: basic bread

Weight: approx. 1 kg/2.2 lb

Put all the ingredients in the machine's bread pan in the listed order. Choose the setting and the crust colour. Start the machine. At the end of the cycle, remove the bread from the pan and set on a rack to cool.

Ingredients

- 400 ml/13 ⅓ fl oz/1 ⅔ d filtered water
- 1 tsp table salt
- 1 tsp organic whole cane sugar
- 435 g/15 ⅓ oz/3 ¾ c organic super strong (high-gluten) flour
- 200 g/7 oz/1 ½ c organic strong brown flour (81% extaction) or light wheat flour
- 150 g/5 ¼ oz/1 c dried figs, soaked
- 1 packet instant yeast

/ This sweet breat can be eaten at the end of a meal with a quality cream dessert, or it can be savoured alone, as a snack. It is rich in soluble fiblre, and favours digestion if eaten regularly. You can also serve it with savoury flavours such as Bayonne ham. /

For:

lazy intestines
athletes
when you feel peckish

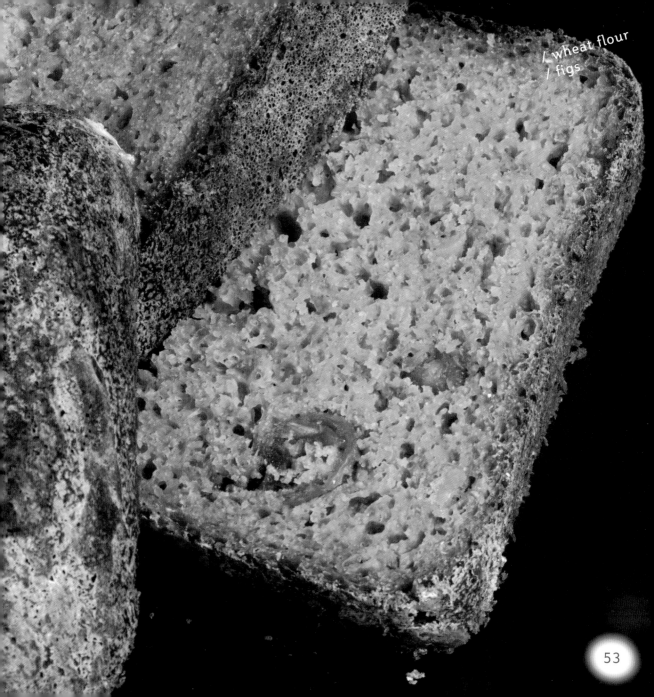

wheat flour
/ figs

/ Mineral-Rich Bread /

Setting: French bread

Weight: approx. 800 g/1 ¾ lb

Put all the ingredients in the machine's bread pan in the listed order. Choose the setting and the crust colour. Start the machine. At the end of the cycle, remove the bread from the pan and set on a rack to cool.

Ingredients

- 350 ml/12 fl oz/1 ½ c spelt-rice-hazelnut drink
- 1 tsp organic canola oil
- 15 g/1 tsp acacia honey
- 1 ½ tsp *fleur de sel* or fine sea salt
- 470 g/16 ½ oz/3 ¾ c organic super strong (high-gluten) flour
- 100 g/3 ½ oz/¾ c organic chestnut flour
- 1 packet instant yeast

/ This delicious, sweet, moist bread is excellent for breakfast and for snacks. The liquid used is rich in minerals and fibre and gives this bread an additional nutritional touch for regulating the digestion. This action is strengthened by the chestnut flour, which is rich in magnesium and potassium. /

For:

athletes
food lovers
lazy intestines

/ wheat flour
/ chestnut flour

55

/ Nighttime Bread /

Setting: sweet bread

Weight: approx. 800 g/1 ¾ lb

Put all the ingredients in the machine's bread pan in the listed order. Choose the setting and the crust colour. Start the machine. At the end of the cycle, remove the bread from the pan and set on a rack to cool.

Ingredients

- 200 ml/6 ⅔ fl oz/⅘ c fresh organic half-cream milk
- 2 bags of calm night herb tea (lime blossom, orange flower, camomile), infused in the warm milk
- 125 ml/4 ⅛ fl oz/½ c filtered water
- 20 g/⅔ oz/4 tsp organic churn butter
- 1 tsp table salt
- 2 ½ tbsp acacia honey
- 400 g/14 oz/3 ½ c organic super strong (high-gluten) flour
- 200 g/7 oz/1 ½ c organic strong whole meal flour, 95% extraction (dark whole wheat flour)
- 1 packet instant yeast

/ This sweet bread is perfect for the evening. You can eat it with herb tea or a glass of milk. Several factors make this a real sleep preparer: it is natually rich in carbohydrades, lime blossom and camomille have calming relaxing effects, and tryptophan is an amino acid found in milk that is a precurser to serotonin. /

För:

insomniacs
children
everyone
calm nights

/ wheat flour
/ milk
/ herb tea

57

/ Rice Bread /

Setting: basic bread

Weight: approx. 850 g/1 lb 14 oz

Put all the ingredients in the machine's bread pan in the listed order. Choose the setting and the crust colour. Start the machine. At the end of the cycle, remove the bread from the pan and set on a rack to cool.

Ingredients

- 300 ml/10 fl oz/1 ¼ c almond milk
- 50 g/1 ¾ oz/generous ¼ c uncooked rice, cooked and then drained
- 70 g/2 ½ oz/1 generous tbsp maple syrup
- 1 tsp table salt
- 1 pinch ground cinnamon
- 200 g/7 oz/1 ½ c organic corn meal
- 320 g/11 ¼ oz/2 ⅝ c organic super strong (high-gluten) flour
- 30 g/1 oz/¼ c sunflower seeds
- 1 packet instant yeast

/ This bread is golden in colour, with a subtle cinnamon and maple syrup flavour. It provides a good amount of energy, useful for athletes, and can also be eaten by anyone for breakfast, snack or when feeling hungry, because it provides an interesting alternative to overly fatty and sugar-filled snacks. The almond milk adds a noteworthy quantity of calcium. /

For:

athletes
when you feel peckish
snack or lunch

/ wheat flour
/ maple syrup
/ almond milk
/ rice

59

/ Wine Bread /

Setting: basic bread

Weight: approx. 750 g/1 ⅔ lb

Put all the ingredients in the machine's bread pan in the listed order. Choose the setting and the crust colour. Start the machine. At the end of the cycle, remove the bread from the pan and set on a rack to cool.

Ingredients

- 200 ml/6 ⅔ fl oz/⅘ c good quality red wine
- 1 tsp table salt
- 1 tsp organic whole cane sugar
- 1 tbsp organic canola oil
- 80 g/2 ⅘ oz/¼ c organic, pitted prunes, in pieces
- 50 g/1 ¾ oz/⅓ c chopped hazelnuts
- 300 g/10 ½ oz/2 ½ c organic strong brown flour (81% extaction) or light wheat flour
- 150 g/5 ¼ oz/1 ⅜ c organic super strong (high-gluten) flour
- 1 packet instant yeast

/ This bread has an original colour and sweet taste that work perfectly as a dessert with a dairy product. It is rich in soluble fibre (prunes) and insoluble fibre (strong brown flour), and will contribute to stimulating lazy intestines. The hazelnuts provide a good supplement of omega-3. This is a delightful, delicious bread that also works as an hors-d'oeuvre. /

For:
food lovers
lazy intestines
dessert

/ wheat flour
/ prunes
/ hazelnuts
/ wine

61

/ Rice-Almond Bread /

Setting: sweet bread

Weight: approx. 1 kg/2.2 lb

Put all the ingredients in the machine's bread pan in the listed order. Choose the setting and the crust colour. Start the machine. At the end of the cycle, remove the bread from the pan and set on a rack to cool.

Ingredients

- 470 ml/15 ⅘ fl oz/2 c organic rice-almond drink
- 3 tbsp organic whole cane sugar
- 30 g/1 oz/scant ¼ c ground almonds
- 400 g/14 oz/3 ½ c organic strong brown flour (81% extaction) or light wheat flour
- 200 g/7 oz/1 ½ c organic super strong (high-gluten) flour
- 150 g/5 ¼ oz/1 c whole, shelled salted almonds
- 1 packet instant yeast

/ Almonds are rich in calcium and can be a good alternative to dairy products. They give this bread plant-based monounsaturated fat and minerals such as magnesium and phosphorus. the rice drink contains carbohydrates that give this bread a special sweetness. /

For:

children
lactose-intolerance

/ Salt-Free Morning Bread /

Setting: basic bread

Weight: approx. 1 kg/2.2 lb

Put all the ingredients in the machine's bread pan in the listed order. Choose the setting and the crust colour. Start the machine. At the end of the cycle, remove the bread from the pan and set on a rack to cool.

Ingredients

- 320 ml/10 ⅘ fl oz/1 ⅓ c Chinese Toucha tea with ginseng
- 1 tsp chestnut honey
- 10 g/⅓ oz/2 tsp organic churn butter
- 550 g/1 lb 4 oz/4 ⅜ c organic strong brown flour (81% extaction) or light wheat flour
- 40 g/1 ½ oz/1 tbsp each sunflower seeds, flaxseed and poppy seeds
- 25 g/scant 1 oz/¼ c meusli
- 1 packet instant yeast

/ This salt-free bread is ideal for people who want to decrease their overall sodium intake. All its ingredients can be found in a balanced breakfast. It is especially recommended for people in a hurry in the morning, because it contributes to a complete, balanced diet. Eat it with a piece of fruit and a dairy product. /

For:

high blood pressure
people in a hurry

/ Orange-Soy Bread /

Setting: sweet bread

Weight: approx. 800 g/1 ¾ lb

Put all the ingredients in the machine's bread pan in the listed order. Choose the setting and the crust colour. Start the machine. At the end of the cycle, remove the bread from the pan and set on a rack to cool.

Ingredients

- 335 ml/11 ⅓ fl oz/1⅖ c calcium-enriched organic soy milk
- 1 tea bag orange-verbena herb tea, infused in the soy milk
- 3 tbsp organic whole cane sugar
- 2 tsp organic soy oil
- 1 tsp table salt
- 20 ml/⅔ fl oz/4 tsp orange-flower water
- 600 g/1 lb 5 oz/4⅘ c organic strong brown flour (81% extaction) or light wheat flour
- 1 packet instant yeast

/ The combination of orange-flower water and the herb tea give this bread a pleasent aroma. The soy milk, preferably calcium-enriched, can replace milk and provide the body with phytoestrogens. In addition, it has no lactose and no cholesterol, and provides plant proteins. Soy oil is perfectly adapted to the body because of its balance in terms of fatty acids (it has ideal proportions of omega-6 and omega-3), making this bread intensely nutritional. /

For:

menopaused women
lactose intolerance

/ wheat flour
/ soy milk
/ orange-flower
water

/ Cinammon Bread /

Setting: sweet bread

Weight: approx. 800 g/1 ¾ lb

Ingredients

- 330 ml/11 ⅕ fl oz/1 ⅖ c filtered water
- 1 tsp *fleur de sel* or fine sea salt
- 2 tbsp organic canola oil
- 2 tbsp organic hemp oil
- 3 tbsp organic whole cane sugar
- 110 g/scant 4 oz/⅞ c multigrain flour
- 400 g/14 oz/3 ½ c organic strong brown flour (81% extaction) or light wheat flour
- 80 g/2 ⅘ oz/⅝ c very strong 100% whole wheat flour
- 4 tbsp ground cinammon
- 1 packet instant yeast

Put all the ingredients in the machine's bread pan in the listed order. Choose the setting and the crust colour. Start the machine. At the end of the cycle, remove the bread from the pan and set on a rack to cool.

/ Cinammon gives this bread a specific colour and a pleasent taste: it goes perfectly with tea. Cinammon is the bark of the cinammon tree and is rich in antioxydants. It helps fight against free radicals and contains fibre. /

For:

food lovers
snack

/ wheat flour
/ multigrain flour
/ cinammon

67

/ Milk Bread /

Setting: French bread

Weight: approx. 750 g/1 ⅔ lb

Put all the ingredients in the machine's bread pan in the listed order. Choose the setting and the crust colour. Start the machine. At the end of the cycle, remove the bread from the pan and set on a rack to cool.

Ingredients

- 210 ml/7 fl oz/¾ c plus 2 tbsp organic half cream milk
- 1 organic sheep's milk yogurt
- 1 ½ tsp table salt
- 2 tbsp first cold pressed organic extra virgin olive oil
- juice of ½ lemon
- 500 g/18 oz/4 c organic strong brown flour (81% extaction) or light wheat flour
- 1 packet instant yeast

/ The milk and the yogurt in this bread make it moist and perfect for breakfast or snack. It is interesting for its calcium content, and is recommended for children, the elderly and people who eat little milk and few dairy products. It is possible to play with different types of milk and yogurt: sheep's milk, goat's milk, sheep's milk yogurt, cow's milk yogurt, etc. /

For:

children
the elderly

/ wheat flour
/ sheep's milk
yogurt
/ milk

69

/ Fruit Bread /

Setting: sweet bread

Weight: approx. 1 kg/2.2 lb

Ingredients

- 300 ml/10 fl oz/1 ¼ c filtered water
- 1 ½ tsp *fleur de sel* or fine sea salt
- 1 tbsp acacia honey
- 2 ½ tbsp organic powdered half-cream milk
- 2 tbsp organic churn butter, melted
- 500 g/18 oz/4 c organic super strong (high-gluten) flour
- 300 g/10 ½ oz/1 ½ c mixed fruit: ½ banana, ½ pear, ½ apple and grapes
- 1 packet instant yeast

Put all the ingredients in the machine's bread pan in the listed order. Choose the setting and the crust colour. Start the machine. At the end of the cycle, remove the bread from the pan and set on a rack to cool.

/ This bread is slightly sweet, thanks to the honey and mixed fresh fruit, which provide simple carbohydrates that give you readily available energy; the chosen flour provides more complex carbohydrates. You can vary the flavours of this bread by replacing part or all of the water with fruit juice, preferably 100% pure juice. It is ideal for breakfast. People with delicate digestive tracts should seed the grapes. /

For:
    athletes
    children

/ Meusli Bread /

Setting: whole grain bread

Weight: approx. 1 kg/2.2 lb

Ingredients

- 325 ml/11 fl oz/1 ⅓ c filtered water
- 1 ½ tsp *fleur de sel* or fine sea salt
- 2 ½ tbsp organic sunflower oil
- 2 tsp organic whole cane sugar
- 400 g/14 oz/3 ½ c super strong (high-gluten) flour
- 150 g/5 ¼ oz/1 ¼ c organic mixed grain flour
- 50 g/1 ¾ oz/⅜ c organic strong whole meal flour, 95% extraction (dark whole wheat flour)
- 40 g/1 ½ oz/½ c chopped almonds, walnuts and hazelnuts
- 2 dried figs, chopped
- 2 prunes, chopped
- 20 raisins
- 50 g/1 ¾ oz/generous ⅓ c sunflower seeds, squash seeds and flaxseed
- 1 packet instant yeast

Put all the ingredients in the machine's bread pan in the listed order. Choose the setting and the crust colour. Start the machine. At the end of the cycle, remove the bread from the pan and set on a rack to cool.

/ This bread is perfectly adapted to breakfast thanks to its complex carbohydrates. It is also very intersting due to the good quality fatty acids found in the seeds, and the simple carbohydrates found in the dried fruit. /

For:
athletes
the morning

/ Potassium Bread /

Setting: basic bread

Weight: approx. 1.1 kg/2.4 lb

Put all the ingredients in the machine's bread pan in the listed order. Choose the setting and the crust colour. Start the machine. At the end of the cycle, remove the bread from the pan and set on a rack to cool.

Ingredients

- 350 ml12 fl oz/1 ½ c filtered water
- 1 ½ tbsp first cold pressed organic extra virgin olive oil
- 1 ½ tsp *fleur de sel* or fine sea salt
- 1 scant tsp acacia honey
- 450 g/1 lb/3 ⅝ c organic super strong (high-gluten) flour
- 150 g/5 ¼ oz/1 ¼ c organic chestnut flour
- 100 g/3 ½ oz dark chocolate (minimum 70% cocoa solids)
- 35 g/1 oz/¼ c pistachios
- 100 g/3 ½ oz/½ c fresh banana
- 1 packet instant yeast

/ This autumn bread has an original brown colour and is very rich in magnesium and potassium. Dark chocolate (at least 70% cocoa solids) mixed with banana and pistachio makes for a subtle blend that gives this bread its delicate flavour. With its sweet flavour, you can eat it like a cake, but it remains nutritionally interesting because it is has less sugar and fat than cakes do. /

For:

children
food lovers
athletes

/ chestnut flour
/ chocolate
/ banana
/ pistachios

73

/ Coconut-Almond Bread /

Put all the ingredients in the machine's bread pan in the listed order. Choose the setting and the crust colour. Start the machine. At the end of the cycle, remove the bread from the pan and set on a rack to cool.

Ingredients

- 330 ml/11 ⅕ fl oz/1 ⅖ c filtered water
- 1 ½ cc tsp *fleur de sel* or fine sea salt
- 2 tbsp first cold pressed organic walnut oil
- 40 g/1 ½ oz/2 ½ tbsp organic whole cane sugar
- 240 g/8 ½ oz/1 ⅞ c very strong 100% whole wheat flour
- 360 g/12 ⅔ oz/2 ⅞ c organic super strong (high–gluten) flour
- 60 g/2 oz/¾ c grated Ceylan coconut
- 45 g/1 ½ oz/⅓ c ground almonds
- 1 packet instant yeast

/ This light whole wheat bread has a very rich, crunchy flavour that goes well both with breakfast and for snack. The combination of coco-nut and walnut oil makes a balance of fatty acids. In addition, it is rich in fibre, iron and antioxydants, thanks to the zinc and selenium found in the almonds. /

For:
athletes
everyone

/ wheat flour
/ coconut
/ almonds

/ Rum Raisin Bread /

Setting: basic bread

Weight: approx. 800 g/1 ¾ lb

Put all the ingredients in the machine's bread pan in the listed order. Choose the setting and the crust colour. Start the machine. At the end of the cycle, remove the bread from the pan and set on a rack to cool.

Ingredients

- 300 ml/10 fl oz/1 ¼ c filtered water
- 1 tbsp dark rum
- 30 g/1 oz/2 tbsp organic churn butter
- 1 ½ tbsp acacia honey
- 1 tsp table salt
- 500 g/18 oz/4 c organic strong brown flour (81% extaction) or light wheat flour
- 40 g/1 ½ oz/⅓ c chopped walnuts
- 60 g/2 oz/½ c raisins
- 1 packet instant yeast

/ This bread has a slightly exotic flavour and can easily replace cake, making for a much more nutritional snack. The walnuts and raisins provide fibre and good fatty acids. And there are no effects of the alcohol: it evaporates when cooked and only the flavour remains. This bread is excellent served with a custard sauce. /

For:
athletes
food lovers

/ wheat flour
/ rum
/ raisins

77

/ Coffee-Chocolate Bread /

Setting: basic bread
and dark crust

Weight: approx. 750 g/1 ⅔ lb

Put all the ingredients in the machine's bread pan in the listed order. Choose the setting and the crust colour. Start the machine. At the end of the cycle, remove the bread from the pan and set on a rack to cool.

Ingredients

- 220 ml/7 ⅖ fl oz/¾ c plus 2 ½ tbsp organic vanilla-flavoured soy milk
- 140 ml/4 ¾ fl oz/⅔ c strong fair-trade coffee
- 2 tbsp instant chicory
- 1 tsp table salt
- 3 tbsp organic whole cane sugar
- 300 g/10 ½ oz/2 ⅜ c organic 85% extraction whole wheat flour
- 250 g/9 oz/2 c organic mixed grain flour
- 2 tbsp cocoa powder
- 1 packet instant yeast

/ This dark brown bread is ideal for breakfast. It is a stimulant, rich in fibre and magnesium, and complex carbohydrates. It has everything you need to get the day off to a good start. /

For:

the morning rush
breakfast lovers
lactose intolerance

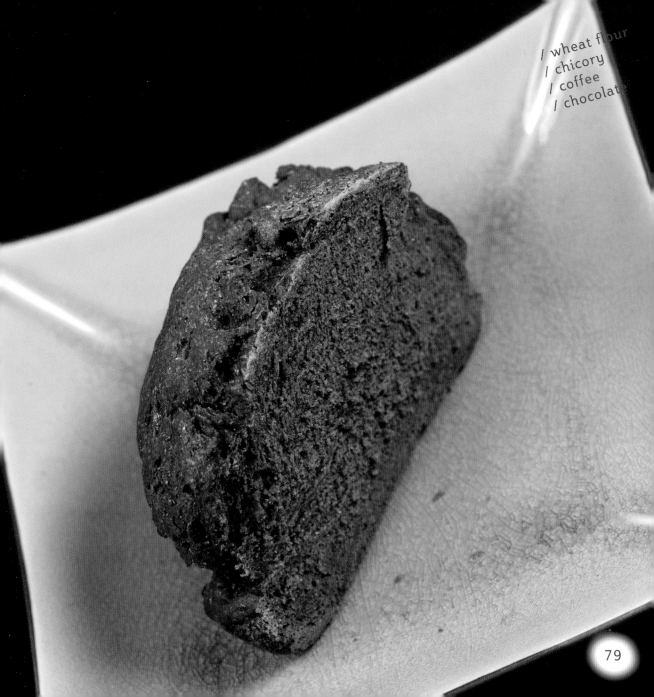

/ Blueberry Bread /

Setting: basic bread

Weight: approx. 800 g/1 ¾ lb

Put all the ingredients in the machine's bread pan in the listed order. Choose the setting and the crust colour. Start the machine. At the end of the cycle, remove the bread from the pan and set on a rack to cool.

Ingredients

- 300 ml/10 fl oz/1 ¼ c filtered water
- 3 tbsp sugar
- 1 tsp table salt
- 20 g/⅔ oz/4 tsp organic churn butter
- 450 g/1 lb/3 ⅝ c organic super strong (high-gluten) flour
- 150 g/5 ¼ oz/1 ½ c fresh or frozen blueberries
- 1 packet instant yeast

/ This bread is very colourful and flavourful. Although not to be eaten every day, it does goes well with lunch or a summer snack. Its blue colour results from being rich in antioxydants—polyphenols including anthocyanin—which are found in blueberries. It is, as a result, an excellent preventive healthfood. You can replace the sugar with violet sugar to add an additional aroma. /

For:

originality
health
everyone

/ Kiwi-Pineapple Bread /

Setting: sweet bread

Weight: approx. 1 kg/2.2 lb

Put all the ingredients in the machine's bread pan in the listed order. Choose the setting and the crust colour. Start the machine. At the end of the cycle, remove the bread from the pan and set on a rack to cool.

Ingredients

- 300 ml/10 fl oz/1 ¼ c almond milk
- 150 ml/5 fl oz/⅔ c filtered water
- 1 tsp acacia honey
- 1 tsp table salt
- 250 g/9 oz/2 c organic strong brown flour (81% extaction) or light wheat flour
- 300 g/10 ½ oz/2 ⅜ c organic super strong (high-gluten) flour
- 75 g/2 ½ oz dried kiwi pieces
- 75 g/2 ½ oz dried banana pieces
- 1 packet instant yeast

/ This slightly sweet dried fruit bread can be eaten for dessert. It is rich in calcium, and the use of almond milk means that people intolerant to the lactose found in cow's milk can eat this bread with, for example a sheep's milk product. Its soluble fibre helps digestion. /

For:

intolerance to cow's milk
light meals
dessert

/ Raisin-Date-Banana Bread /

Setting: French Bread

Weight: approx. 900 g/2 lb

Put all the ingredients in the machine's bread pan in the listed order. Choose the setting and the crust colour. Start the machine. At the end of the cycle, remove the bread from the pan and set on a rack to cool.

Ingredients

- 200 ml/6⅔ fl oz/⅘ c calcium-enriched organic soy milk
- 150 ml/5 fl oz/⅔ c filtered water
- 1 tsp table salt
- 1 ½ tbsp rhododendron honey
- 5 g/1 tsp natural vanilla flavour
- 600 g/1 lb 5 oz/4⅘ c organic 85% extraction whole wheat flour
- 50 g/1 ¾ oz/⅓ c organic sultanas
- 50 g/1 ¾ oz/⅓ c medjool dates pieces
- 50 g/1 ¾ oz/⅓ c organic dried banana pieces
- 1 packet instant yeast

/ This high-energy bread is ideal for athletes, children and active people, but also to start the day, at snack or to recuperate after doing some exercise. The dried fruit, dates, raisins and bananas provide simple carbohydrates, which are very well assimilated by the body, and also potassium and magnesium. Rhododendron honey, in addition to its stimulant and healing properties, was chosen because it is only collected at high altitudes, preserving it from contamination and pollution. /

For:

athletes
children
active people

/ wheat flour
/ banana
/ raisins
/ dates

83

/ Chocolate-Banana Bread /

Setting: basic bread

Weight: approx. 1 kg/2.2 lb

Put all the ingredients in the machine's bread pan in the listed order. Choose the setting and the crust colour. Start the machine. At the end of the cycle, remove the bread from the pan and set on a rack to cool.

Ingredients

- 100 ml/3 $^1/_3$ fl oz/$^2/_5$ c filtered water
- 250 ml/8 ½ fl oz/1 c calcium-enriched organic soy milk
- 40 to 60 g/1 ½ to 2 oz organic chocolate spread
- 1 tsp table salt
- 3 tbsp fair-trade cane sugar
- 400 g/14 oz/3 ½ c organic multigrain flour
- 200 g/7 oz/1 ½ c organic soft (pastry) flour
- 100 g/3 ½ oz/$^2/_3$ c organic dried banana
- 1 packet instant yeast
- 40 to 60 g/1 ½ to 2 oz chocolate chips (optional)

/ This bread has a subtle mixture of banana and chocolate that delights the taste buds. Its nutritional density is that much more interesting than a cake because it has less fat and sugar and more interesting minerals (calcium, potassium, magnesium). /

For:

children
food lovers
lactose intolerance

/ mixed grain flour
/ soy milk
/ chocolate
/ banana

/ Quince Bread /

Setting: sweet bread

Weight: approx. 800 g/1 ¾ lb

Put all the ingredients in the machine's bread pan in the listed order. Choose the setting and the crust colour. Start the machine. At the end of the cycle, remove the bread from the pan and set on a rack to cool.

Ingredients

- 330 ml/11 ⅕ fl oz/1 ⅖ c filtered water
- 20 g/⅔ oz/4 tsp organic churn butter
- 1 tsp table salt
- 1 tbsp lavender honey
- 500 g/18 oz/4 c organic super strong (high-gluten) flour
- 100 g/3 ½ oz homemade quince paste
- 1 packet instant yeast

/ This autumn bread sweetened with honey and quince paste can be savoured both for breakfast and for snack. Quinces are rich in soluble fibres such as pectin which, when combined with tannin, has anti-diarrheal properties. This pretty autumn fruit can also be cooked with certain meat and, notably, poultry. /

For:
children
fast intestines

/ wheat flour
/ quince paste

/ Tick-Tock Bread /

Setting: basic bread

Weight: approx. 800 g/1 ¾ lb

Put all the ingredients in the machine's bread pan in the listed order. Choose the setting and the crust colour. Start the machine. At the end of the cycle, remove the bread from the pan and set on a rack to cool.

Ingredients

- 330 ml/11 ⅕ fl oz/1 ⅖ c filtered water
- 2 tsp first cold pressed organic hazelnut oil
- 1 ½ tsp *fleur de sel* or fine sea salt
- 1 ½ tbsp chestnut honey
- 600 g/1 lb 5 oz/4 ⅘ c organic super strong (high-gluten) flour
- 60 g/2 oz/½ c fresh hazelnuts
- 1 packet instant yeast

/ This bread has a subtle praline flavour that is ideal for breakfast and snacks. Hazelnuts and hazelnut oil contain monounsaturated fatty acids that are good for the cardiovascular system, like olive oil. In addition, they have flavonoids and vitamin E, which are known for their antioxydant properties. Try this bread with dark chocolate: the association is nutritionally much better for the health than some well known spreads! /

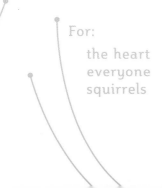

For:

the heart
everyone
squirrels

/ Banana-Sesame Bread /

Setting: basic bread

Weight: approx. 800 g/1 ¾ lb

Put all the ingredients in the machine's bread pan in the listed order. Choose the setting and the crust colour. Start the machine. At the end of the cycle, remove the bread from the pan and set on a rack to cool.

Ingredients

- 200 ml/6 ⅔ fl oz/⅘ c calcium-enriched organic soy milk
- 150 ml/5 fl oz/⅔ c filtered water
- 1.5 tbsp acacia honey
- 1 tsp salt
- 350 g/12 ⅓ oz/2 ⅞ c organic strong brown flour (81% extaction) or light wheat flour
- 150 g/5 ¼ oz/¾ c organic semolina
- 30 g/1 oz/scant ¼ c sesame seeds
- 120 g/4 ¼ oz/1 scant c organic dried banana pieces
- 1 packet instant yeast

/ This breakfast and snack bread is rich is slowly assimilated complex carbohydrates and is therefore good for athletes to rebuild their energy reserves. In addition, the bananas provide potassium, which is often missing in people's diets, and sesame oil provides a supplement of essential fatty acids. This bread can also be eaten by people who are intolerant to cow's milk. In this case, you can serve it with sheep's milk cottage cheese, for example. /

For:

intolerance to cow's milk
athletes
snack or breakfast

/ wheat flour
/ soy milk
/ sesame
/ banana

/ Canadian Bread /

Setting: sweet bread

Weight: approx. 800 g/1 ¾ lb

Put all the ingredients in the machine's bread pan in the listed order. Choose the setting and the crust colour. Start the machine. At the end of the cycle, remove the bread from the pan and set on a rack to cool.

Ingredients

- 200 ml/6 ⅔ fl oz/⅘ c soy or almond milk
- 100 ml/3 ⅓ fl oz/⅖ c filtered water
- 1 tsp table salt
- 50 g/1 ¾ oz/1 scant tbsp maple syrup
- 300 g/10 ½ oz/3 ⅛ c organic strong brown flour (81% extaction) or light wheat flour
- 200 g/7 oz/1 ½ c organic super strong (high-gluten) flour
- 100 g/3 ½ oz/¾ c organic meusli soaked in 100 ml/3 ¹/₃ fl oz/⅖ c milk and then drained
- 1 packet instant yeast

/ This sweet bread has a delicate maple syrup flavour and is ideal for snacks and breakfast. It is rich in complex carbohydrates and fibre, from the meusli, and as a result is a perfect energy supply for children and athletes. Made with almond milk, it provides a good quantity of calcium. /

For:

children
athletes
breakfast or snack

/ wheat flour
/ maple syrup
/ plant milk
/ meusli

93

Problems and solutions

If you encounter problems, try increasing or decreasing the amount of one of the ingredients, as indicated below. Only make one change at a time, in order to determine the exact effect it has on your recipe, which will depend on your machine.

The bread caves in and is hollow or mushrooms
- Liquid: Reduce the amount of liquid by 1 tablespoon. After about 10 minutes of kneading, the pan should be clean and the dough soft and smooth. If it is too humid, add flour spoonful by spoonful, waiting between each addition, until you get the consistency you are looking for.
- Yeast: Reduce the amount of yeast by ¼ teaspoon.
- Sugar: Reduce the amount of sugar by 1 teaspoon (note that if you add fruit, you increase the amount of sugar).
- Salt: Increase the amount of salt by ¼ teaspoon (the minimum amount of salt required is ½ teaspoon for 450 g/1 lb/3½ c flour).

The bread has a rough surface
- Liquid: Increase the amount of liquid 1 tablespoon at a time, waiting between each addition, until you get the consistency you are looking for.
- Gluten: Reduce the amount of non-bread flour, replacing it with bread flour.
- Additional ingredients: Reduce the amount of supplementary ingredients used.

The bread does not rise enough
- Yeast: Check that the yeast you are using is still good. Be careful that the yeast does not come into contact with the salt in the bread pan. Increase the quantity of yeast by ¼ teaspoon.
- Liquid: Increase the amount of liquid 1 tablespoon at a time, waiting between each addition, until you get the consistency you are looking for.
- Salt: Decrease the amount of salt by ¼ teaspoon.
- Sugar: Increase the amount of sugar by 1 teaspoon.
- Additional ingredients: Reduce the amount of supplementary ingredients used.

The bread too toasted
- Sugar: Decrease the amount of sugar by 1 teaspoon.
- Fat: Reduce the amount of fat by 1 teaspoon.
- Crust colour: If you chose a dark crust, choose a lighter setting.

Recipe index

The author expresses sincere thanks to the
"bakers", all dieticians and nutritionists, who
participated in writing this book.
Stéphane Bloch
Camille Joly
Frédéric Capel

Editorial director / Marie-Alexandre Perraud
Editing / Agnès Carayon
Graphic design / Maevi Colomina & Romain Pages Publishing
Photography / Valentin and Jean-Pierre Duval
Translation / Anne Trager
Printing and binding / Delo Tiskarna, Slovenia, Europe
First published in French in 2007, by Romain Pages Editions, France.

ISBN no. 978-1-906909-08-6

Romain Pages Publishing
Lincoln House
300 High Holborn
WC1V 7JH - London
United Kingdom
enquiries@romain-pages.co.uk
www.romain-pages.co.uk

Romain Pages Editions
BP 82030
30252 Sommières cedex
France
e.mail : contact@romain-pages.com
www.romain-pages.com